Apostasy

by Gino DiIorio

A Samuel French Acting Edition

New York Hollywood London Toronto

SAMUELFRENCH.COM

Copyright © 2009 by Gino DiIorio

ALL RIGHTS RESERVED

CAUTION: Professionals and amateurs are hereby warned that *APOSTASY* is subject to a royalty. It is fully protected under the copyright laws of the United States of America, the British Commonwealth, including Canada, and all other countries of the Copyright Union. All rights, including professional, amateur, motion picture, recitation, lecturing, public reading, radio broadcasting, television and the rights of translation into foreign languages are strictly reserved. In its present form the play is dedicated to the reading public only.

The amateur live stage performance rights to *APOSTASY* are controlled exclusively by Samuel French, Inc., and royalty arrangements and licenses must be secured well in advance of presentation. PLEASE NOTE that amateur royalty fees are set upon application in accordance with your producing circumstances. When applying for a royalty quotation and license please give us the number of performances intended, dates of production, your seating capacity and admission fee. Royalties are payable one week before the opening performance of the play to Samuel French, Inc., at 45 W. 25th Street, New York, NY 10010.

Royalty of the required amount must be paid whether the play is presented for charity or gain and whether or not admission is charged.

Stock royalty quoted upon application to Samuel French, Inc.

For all other rights than those stipulated above, apply to: Elaine Devlin Literary, Inc. 20 West 23rd Street, 3rd Floor, New York, NY 10010 Attn: Elaine Devlin.

Particular emphasis is laid on the question of amateur or professional readings, permission and terms for which must be secured in writing from Samuel French, Inc.

Copying from this book in whole or in part is strictly forbidden by law, and the right of performance is not transferable.

Whenever the play is produced the following notice must appear on all programs, printing and advertising for the play: "Produced by special arrangement with Samuel French, Inc."

Due authorship credit must be given on all programs, printing and advertising for the play.

ISBN 978-0-573-69608-4   Printed in U.S.A.   #29001

No one shall commit or authorize any act or omission by which the copyright of, or the right to copyright, this play may be impaired.

No one shall make any changes in this play for the purpose of production.

Publication of this play does not imply availability for performance. Both amateurs and professionals considering a production are strongly advised in their own interests to apply to Samuel French, Inc., for written permission before starting rehearsals, advertising, or booking a theatre.

No part of this book may be reproduced, stored in a retrieval system, or transmitted in any form, by any means, now known or yet to be invented, including mechanical, electronic, photocopying, recording, videotaping, or otherwise, without the prior written permission of the publisher.

MUSIC NOTE

Licensees are solely responsible for obtaining formal written permission from copyright owners to use copyrighted music in the performance of this play and are strongly cautioned to do so. If no such permission is obtained by the licensee, then the licensee must use only original music that the licensee owns and controls. Licensees are solely responsible and liable for all music clearances and shall indemnify the copyright owners of the play and their licensing agent, Samuel French, Inc., against any costs, expenses, losses and liabilities arising from the use of music by licensees.

IMPORTANT BILLING AND CREDIT REQUIREMENTS

All producers of *APOSTASY must* give credit to the Author of the Play in all programs distributed in connection with performances of the Play, and in all instances in which the title of the Play appears for the purposes of advertising, publicizing or otherwise exploiting the Play and/or a production. The name of the Author *must* appear on a separate line on which no other name appears, immediately following the title and *must* appear in size of type not less than fifty percent of the size of the title type.

APOSTASY was first produced on July 15, 2006 at the New Jersey Repertory Theatre.

SHEILA	Susan G. Bob
DR. JULIUS STRONG	Evander Duck Jr.
RACHEL	Natalie Wilder

Directed by SuzAnne Barabas
Set design by Carrie Mossman
Lighting design by Jill Nagle
Sound design by Merek Royce Press
Costume design by Patricia E. Doherty
Stage Managere by Rose Riccardi
Properties by Jessica Parks

APOSTASY received its New York premiere on March 15, 2007 at the Urban Stages Theatre.

SHEILA	Susan Greenhill
RACHEL	Susan Louise O'Conner
DR. JULIUS STRONG	Harrold Surratt

Directed by Frances Hill
Set design by Roman Tatarowicz
Costume design by Nadia Fadeeva
Lighting design by Josh Bradford
Video design by William Cusick
Sound design by David Margolin Lawson
Stage managed by Carol A. Sullivan

CHARACTERS

SHEILA GOLD – An attractive woman in her 50s. She suffers from terminal cancer and has decided to spend her last days at a hospice. She was a successful businesswoman and can be difficult to deal with.

RACHEL GOLD – Her daughter, a plain woman in her 30s, almost the exact antithesis of her mother. She has worked at Planned Parenthood for five years and believes she is a disappointment to her mother.

DR. JULIUS STRONG – He is a dashing black man in his early 50s. He wears a sharp suit and has a magnetic stare. His smile is constant, but not painted on. Despite the trappings of his profession, there is something endearing about his demeanor

Time

The present

Place

A Hospice

ACT 1

Scene One

(A cottage at a private hospice. It is pleasantly furnished, with assorted New Age trinkets. Whatever warmth the room possesses is forced. But aside from some hospital equipment off to the side, it almost seems like a summer home by a lake. **SHEILA** *sits in bed staring straight out at the audience. Behind her is a huge television screen and on it, we see the face of a passionate televangelist,* **DR. JULIUS STRONG.***)*

DR. JULIUS STRONG. *(V.O.)* Have faith! Brothers and sisters, we have nothing without our faith. The greatest minds the world has ever known, greater minds than I, Albert Einstein, Saint Augustine, they knew that the deeper we go into our knowledge, the more we see the essential nature of faith. Well, you say, Brother Julius, we live in age of reason! Is that so? When your body is tired and broken and you want to give up, it's not reason that gets you out of bed in the morning. When you're certain you cannot take one more step and you're ready to give in to all that limits you, it's not reason that makes you put one foot in front of the other. What is it? It's FAITH, brothers and sister. Faith and reason, hand in hand. If it offends reason it cannot be an article of faith. Faith is the basis of all knowledge. Faith is the road to Jesus Christ. *(pause)* HAVE FAITH. *(He whispers.)* Have faith, and faith will be given to you.

(There is the sound of the knob turning. **SHEILA** *jumps up, shuts the TV and runs into the bathroom. There is a pause and then some knocking.)*

RACHEL. Ma?

SHEILA. *(O.S.)* What?

RACHEL. Are you all right?

SHEILA. *(O.S.)* I'm in the bathroom.

RACHEL. What?

SHEILA. *(O.S.)* I said I'm in the bathroom.

RACHEL. (**RACHEL** *opens the door with her key.*) Why is the door locked?

SHEILA. *(O.S.)* I can't hear you.

RACHEL. Why is the door locked?

SHEILA. *(O.S.)* I lock it sometimes!

RACHEL. Oh. Are you all right?

SHEILA. *(O.S.)* I'll be out in a minute.

RACHEL. This place is a mess.

SHEILA. *(O.S.)* What?

RACHEL. Nothing.

(She takes off her coat and begins cleaning.)

SHEILA *(exiting)* What did you say?

RACHEL. I said this place is a mess.

SHEILA. Oh, don't worry, the cleaning woman straightens up.

RACHEL. I've got some weed for you.

SHEILA. That's good.

RACHEL. And after we smoke this, I've got some muffins.

SHEILA. Lucky me.

RACHEL. Where's your pipe?

SHEILA. On the dresser. Where were you last night?

*(**RACHEL** gathers the pipe and during this, begins prepping the weed.)*

RACHEL. I had to work late.

SHEILA. Why?

RACHEL. We had some last minute issues to deal with.

SHEILA. Like what?

RACHEL. This woman. She was crying cause it was her 7th abortion, okay? Lucky seven. And I tried, as politely as

I could, to explain to her that maybe a different form of birth control would be a legitimate option at this juncture of her life. But then she got all hostile on me. "Who did I think I was, this is my job, I'm supposed to be serving her, blah blah," like it's me, right? And I did something I never did before.

SHEILA. You smacked her.

RACHEL. I should have smacked her. That would have made sense. No, instead, *I* started crying. She's in there, and yelling at me, and I just broke down; like she's beating me up and I'm thanking her for it…like what the hell am I doing here, right? Am I just not cut out for this?

SHEILA. Wait, I thought you were management now.

RACHEL. I am. But we're short counselors as it is and Gabby called in sick, so I had to fill in.

SHEILA. Maybe it's time for a change.

RACHEL. I did change. I took the position.

SHEILA. How long have you been doing this?

RACHEL. Going on five years.

SHEILA. That's a long time to be doing volunteer work.

RACHEL. It's not volunteer. I get paid.

SHEILA. Barely. It sounds like twice the work for the same money.

RACHEL. *(She begins lighting the pipe.)* All right, this is not the response I was looking for. It was just a tough day and –

SHEILA. Why don't you go back to school and get your masters?

RACHEL. Because I don't want to. Smoke this.

SHEILA. But you could be –

(RACHEL sticks the pipe in SHEILA's mouth.)

RACHEL. Get busy.

SHEILA. I'm just asking.

RACHEL. Finish that so you can eat something.

SHEILA. Honey, I just threw up.

RACHEL. You gotta eat.

SHEILA. You're beginning to sound like me.

RACHEL. Just smoke so you'll get an appetite so you'll eat.

SHEILA. Close the window.

RACHEL. Why?

SHEILA. I don't want anyone to smell it.

RACHEL. Who's gonna smell it, the geriatric patrol?

SHEILA. Just do it, please. I don't want to get thrown out.

RACHEL. They're not going to throw you out. The whole place is high as a kite. The only difference is, their drugs are legal. I thought you said they respected your privacy.

SHEILA. Can you please just do what I ask? Just once? Ever since you were a little girl – whoa, what's in this?

RACHEL. I don't know, I had to change dealers. I got from some Haitian guy in the projects. What a neighborhood.

SHEILA. That'll put some hope in your rope. Wow. Maybe you could start a delivery service.

RACHEL. Junkie Jews, we deliver.

SHEILA. This is *much* better than last time. My gosh, I can't feel my tuchus.

RACHEL. The guy said, "dis is some good shit, mon."

SHEILA. Sure is. And who is this guy?

RACHEL. He's a dealer, Ma. I'm not dating him.

SHEILA. Uh-huh. And how *is* the dating scene?

RACHEL. Okay. Any other buttons you'd like to push?

SHEILA. I'm not allowed to ask?

RACHEL. Fine. I had a date Thursday night.

SHEILA. Oh.

RACHEL. It was a freakin' nightmare.

SHEILA. Tell me.

RACHEL. The Titanic meets the Poseidon Adventure.

SHEILA. What happened?

RACHEL. Nooo…

SHEILA. I'll give you a hit of my weed.

RACHEL. That's medicinal.

SHEILA. Take it.

RACHEL. Oh, why not.

(RACHEL takes a hit.)

SHEILA. Tell me the story.

RACHEL. Boy, that is good stuff.

SHEILA. Maybe you should date the dealer.

RACHEL. Okay. Guy was late, and I'm sitting there with the Italian bartender at Pietro's, Joe Bagadoughnuts, or whatever his name is –

SHEILA. *(noticing the "Kubaton" key chain, next to RACHEL's purse)* What's that?

RACHEL. Huh? Nothing, it's a key chain.

SHEILA. What the hell kind of key is that?

RACHEL. It's the style Ma. It sticks out, see? It's easy to find. Do you want to hear this or not?

SHEILA. All right!

RACHEL. Anyway, it's past 9 and I figure I'm getting stood up –

SHEILA. Wait, where did you find this guy?

RACHEL. I found him on "It's A Match." Remember? That Jewish Singles Website thing you bought me for my birthday?

SHEILA. Oh.

RACHEL. Yeah. Couldn't you have given me a book?

SHEILA. So impersonal

RACHEL. I like impersonal. Impersonal is easy.

SHEILA. Whatever. Keep going.

RACHEL. Okay, half past nine, I'm about to leave, when in walks this guy –

SHEILA. And he's drop dead gorgeous.

RACHEL. In – your life.

SHEILA. Come on.

RACHEL. In – your life. Face was chiseled, kinda cute, little scruffy, ripped jean kinda thing, Calgon take me away.

SHEILA. Wow.

RACHEL. I smile at him, he's smiles back, and we're having a moment, for once this is gonna be great. But then, he walks right – by – me. Because he's not meeting me, he's meeting set of tits at the end of the bar. And sure enough, walking right behind him, in the shadow of Mr. Drop Dead Gorgeous, is Mr. Nebbish of the Universe, Norman the Bean Counter with a dead squirrel on his head. THAT's my date.

SHEILA. Why did he have a dead squirrel on his head?

RACHEL. It was a rug Ma! A roadkill rug! And I'm in a panic. I can't go left, can't go right, I'm in his sights, he's got the hand out, winding up the smile, putting on the "charmed to meet you" face, the whole thing. And I'm hoping by some chance miracle my brain implodes or there's a fire drill, but to no avail. Next thing I know I'm stuck talking to Mr. Blind Date and his dead pet squirrel helmet for the next two hours. Like, why me, right?

SHEILA. So you tried it, you meet some people.

RACHEL. I'm 31 years old, I've met enough people.

SHEILA. I'm sorry, I thought it would be a nice gift.

RACHEL. It was. I know your heart was in the right place. Give me a nice gift now and eat something.

(holding a box of muffins)

SHEILA. What's this one?

RACHEL. I think its Apple Banana.

SHEILA. Feels like rubber.

RACHEL. It's fat free.

SHEILA. Why did you get fat free?

RACHEL. They're not all fat free.

SHEILA. Do I look like I need to lose weight?

RACHEL. No, it's just that I thought –

SHEILA. I got cancer eating me from the inside out and you're cutting my calorie intake?

RACHEL. So don't eat that one. Try another.

SHEILA. Oh come on.

RACHEL. (*playfully patronizing*) We have to eat something now.

SHEILA. We have to find you a guy.

RACHEL. We have to get you better.

SHEILA. Please.

RACHEL. Come on, this one is, what's this…corn.

SHEILA. All right.

(**SHEILA** *cuts a piece off and starts to nibble on it.*)

RACHEL. What am I gonna do without you?

SHEILA. (*sings*) "You'll get along without me, very well."

RACHEL. Eat.

SHEILA. This is the best muffin I ever had.

RACHEL. You got the munchies.

SHEILA. Great. I could be one of those articles in True Story. I WAS A HOSPICE JUNKIE. "My daughter got me high – now there's no turning back."

RACHEL. It works.

SHEILA. It does work.

(*She takes a bite.*)

At least for a while. Wait, let me see that key chain.

RACHEL. (*handing it to* **SHEILA**) It's nothing, you can stick it in your jeans.

SHEILA. It's heavy – Oh, I've seen one of these. This is a karate thing.

RACHEL. It's a Kubaton. It's a little –

SHEILA. Like a club. Right? You poke the guy in the eyes with it or something.

RACHEL. Something like that.

SHEILA. What's going on that you need this?

RACHEL. I just thought it'd be good to have. To protect myself. Hey, did I see Josie walking through?

SHEILA. Yes, she's still working here. You do what you have to do I suppose.

RACHEL. Of course. And what exactly does she do?

SHEILA. It's creative visualization, Reiki, whatever it is.

RACHEL. It's a rip off.

SHEILA. It's not a rip off to someone who's run out of choices.

RACHEL. I'm sorry, but –

SHEILA. You don't take away someone's hope. It may be all that they have.

RACHEL. You don't take away their life savings either.

SHEILA. Oh please, she's not getting rich giving those treatments. And you shouldn't judge. You of all people.

RACHEL. What's that supposed to mean?

SHEILA. She's a healer. Do you do any healing?

RACHEL. Planned Parenthood is a legitimate medical establishment.

SHEILA. Teaching prep school drop outs how to put condoms on bananas.

RACHEL. Ma, that is so not true.

SHEILA. You just got through saying you were fed up and you wanted to quit.

RACHEL. I never said that. And most of our patients come from poor neighborhoods. At least I'm not some witch doctor pawning off cures when there aren't any.

*(Pause. **SHEILA** says nothing.)*

Look, just forget it. All right? You want to try a blue berry?

SHEILA. Do you like being the big macher? *(pronounced Mah-ka.)*

RACHEL. It's a different set of problems. Now I answer to the regional manager and she's a walking cliché, "let's try thinking out of the box." I can't even FIND the box, all right? The box got tossed into the compactor. And then we've got security issues…now.

SHEILA. What?

RACHEL. It's nothing. You want butter?

SHEILA. What security issues? What are you talking about?

RACHEL. Nothing. A couple of crackpot phone calls.

SHEILA. So you got this?

(She picks up the kubaton.)

RACHEL. I didn't want to worry you.

SHEILA. I'm you're mother, I worry.

RACHEL. These Pro Life Neo Nazis put out a website giving the addresses of doctors who perform abortions and certain Planned Parenthood addresses. There's no sign, like, "go kill these doctors," but you get the point. It's nothing more than an open invitation to violence, it's a threat. Like there they are, go get them and…our center showed up on the list.

SHEILA. Oh my God.

RACHEL. I knew I shouldn't have told you.

SHEILA. Did you tell the police?

RACHEL. There's not much they can do about it. It's a free speech issue and it's going to court and all this stuff. But everyone is really nervous and –

SHEILA. Well, are you going to hire a security guard or –

RACHEL. We have security. There's surveillance, they even want to monitor my apartment building.

SHEILA. Why?

RACHEL. Cause…just as a precaution.

SHEILA. Are they doing that for everyone?

RACHEL. No, just….okay. My name showed up on the website.

SHEILA. You?

RACHEL. I don't know how they found out so quickly, but you go on and there it is, Center Manager, Rachel

Gold.

SHEILA. Get another job.

RACHEL. I believe in this one.

SHEILA. If anything ever happened to you –

RACHEL. Nothing is going to happen. Don't worry. Besides, you were the one who always told me to take chances, to stand up for what I believed in, right?

SHEILA. This isn't what I had in mind.

RACHEL. All right. Mom, we don't need to get into this again. I'd just like to think when push comes to shove, you would support me.

SHEILA. I do and I'm proud of you.

RACHEL. No, you're not.

SHEILA. I want you to be happy.

RACHEL. You wanted me to take over the business.

SHEILA. Well, it would have been nice if you were more involved –

RACHEL. Seriously, deep down, you're pissed at me because I didn't take over "Sheila's Closet."

SHEILA. If you took over the business then I never would have been able to sell it, now would I?

RACHEL. To be in business you have to be ruthless. You have to lie and cheat –

SHEILA. Not all the time.

RACHEL. To be successful at it you do. Believe me, it would have been a disaster and –

SHEILA. *(overlapping)* I just thought it would have been a –

RACHEL. – I would have been miserable.

SHEILA. – step up for you.

RACHEL. Besides, I saw what that place did to you and everyone else.

SHEILA. What do you mean?

RACHEL. You were never around, Ma.

SHEILA. I was building a business.

RACHEL. Right. At the expense of other things.

SHEILA. You mean my family.

RACHEL. Well, yeah.

SHEILA. You think it's my fault that my marriage failed.

RACHEL. No, it's nobody's fault –

SHEILA. That's why you chose to live with your father –

RACHEL. Here we go. It is not –

SHEILA. You were always closer to him, you always sided with him, and that's why you chose him –

RACHEL. Because you were never there. You were out fourteen hours a day working on the goddamned – (business.)

SHEILA. So you're saying if I was there more often, your father never would have left me.

RACHEL. No, I'm not. But you had your priorities. You put it all into the store and….you didn't need us. As much.

(pause)

Oh come on Ma, this is…Look, you accomplished a lot. And…it's amazing. You really built up something there. It's like, I mean jeez, you made a bundle when you sold it, right?

SHEILA. So?

RACHEL. So…it's quite an accomplishment.

(Trying to change the subject, **RACHEL** *begins cleaning up.)*

Hey, it's a good thing I never took it over. Imagine me selling stuff on line. I wouldn't know where to begin.

SHEILA. At least no one would be trying to kill you. Now would they.

RACHEL. Ma, it's a bunch of crackpots, all right? They're all talk.

(pause)

It smells like a Grateful Dead concert in here.

SHEILA. I've had enough.

RACHEL. You wanna eat some more?

SHEILA. No, put it away.

RACHEL. Do you want to go for a walk?

SHEILA. Maybe later. I'd rather sleep.

RACHEL. Okay. Now, I've got some stuff to do tomorrow morning, but I can swing by around eleven for lunch, okay? That way if we have to build your appetite again, that gives us some time.

SHEILA. You don't have to.

RACHEL. I want to.

SHEILA. But I know you're busy –

RACHEL. Enough, would you? I'm going to leave these in case you're hungry later.

(**RACHEL** *puts the pipe into dresser drawer, and pulls out some brochures.*)

What's this?

SHEILA. Oh let me have those.

RACHEL. "Heritage Church of the Living Christ."

SHEILA. It's nothing.

RACHEL. Where did you get this?

SHEILA. It's nothing. It's some literature I sent away for. It's nothing.

RACHEL. What are you doing with this?

SHEILA. I'm thinking of converting.

RACHEL. What?

SHEILA. To Christianity.

(*Pause.* **RACHEL** *laughs. After a moment,* **SHEILA** *joins her.*)

RACHEL. That's funny.

SHEILA. Yeah.

RACHEL. (*both still laughing*) What the hell is in this weed?

(**SHEILA** *stops laughing.*)

SHEILA. I'm serious.

RACHEL. What.
SHEILA. About converting.
RACHEL. No.
SHEILA. Yeah.
RACHEL. But…you can't.
SHEILA. Why not?
RACHEL. Cause you're Jewish.
SHEILA. I know.
RACHEL. Well…what am *I* gonna do?
SHEILA. You can do whatever you want.
RACHEL. Ma –
SHEILA. It's something I've been thinking about for a long time.
RACHEL. You can't be serious. You bought me a subscription to a Jewish Singles Website so I would find a Jewish guy, right?
SHEILA. I know.
RACHEL. You made me break up with Tony Giamarco because he wasn't Jewish.
SHEILA. You didn't like him.
RACHEL. The hell I didn't.
SHEILA. He ended up in prison.
RACHEL. So what? He was my boyfriend.
SHEILA. It is not a decision I make lightly.
RACHEL. I know, but –
SHEILA. A lot of things have changed.
RACHEL. *(overlapping)* – you're talking about your entire identity? How can you throw away everything you've ever thought about the world?
SHEILA. How do you know what I think about the world?
RACHEL. Ma…
SHEILA. Maybe it's none of your business.
RACHEL. *(overlapping)* How can you say that –
SHEILA *(overlapping)* I don't owe you –

RACHEL *(overlapping)* I don't even –

SHEILA *(overlapping)* – an explanation.

RACHEL. know what to –

SHEILA. It's hard for me to explain it to myself. I just know what I feel and lying here for all this time and taking an account of things, I've been feeling a little differently. That's all. Lately.

RACHEL. *(pause)* Does this mean no brisket on Passover?

SHEILA. I won't even make it to Passover.

RACHEL. Don't say that.

SHEILA. *(pause)* Look at the bright side. Remember when you were in grade school and you felt left out at Christmas? Now you can hang a stocking, too.

RACHEL. So what are you, Born Again?

SHEILA. No, I'm just thinking about it.

RACHEL. Dr. Julius Strong.

SHEILA. He's an evangelist.

RACHEL. Like a Southern Baptist?

SHEILA. No, he's not from the South. There are ministries all over.

RACHEL. Ministries of Heritage Creek, California. Couldn't you at least have run off with some Catholics? At least they got better songs.

SHEILA. They have songs. He has a show, *The Strong Hour*. It's very inspiring.

RACHEL. I'll bet. Don't waste any time asking you for money, do they?

SHEILA. Are you worried about it?

RACHEL. What?

SHEILA. The money.

RACHEL. Of course not. What do you mean?

SHEILA. The money I'm leaving you.

RACHEL. Ma.

SHEILA. I just thought you –

RACHEL. What does the money have to do with it?

SHEILA. Nothing, just –

RACHEL. How can you insult me this way? I don't give a damn about the money, I care about you. Who brought up money? I don't need your money.

SHEILA. Honey, I didn't mean –

RACHEL. What the hell are you talking about?

SHEILA. Nothing. I'm sorry, I got confused.

RACHEL. I was talking about how they were asking for money.

SHEILA. I'm tired.

RACHEL. In the brochure.

*(Pause. **RACHEL** is still in shock over this, not knowing what to say.)*

Okay. Fine. I'll be by tomorrow. Do you need anything?

SHEILA. Rolling papers. I'm kidding.

RACHEL. This is a little hard for me.

SHEILA. I know.

RACHEL. I feel betrayed. I guess.

SHEILA. You shouldn't.

RACHEL. Well, I do.

SHEILA. Okay, you know how I feel? I feel as though I'm at the edge of something and I'm not at all ready to jump. And I need help.

RACHEL. I understand that.

SHEILA. We all know that we're going to die and we spend no time at all preparing for it.

(pause)

Sometimes I sit here and I'm amazed at how empty my heart is. I'm supposed to look back and feel I don't know, fulfilled or a sense of joy and accomplishment. I just look back and feel nothing.

RACHEL. You make me feel bad, how can you say this?

SHEILA. This is not about you; this is about me. The business, everything, it just doesn't seem to be enough. I thought…I don't know what I thought. You come, you visit, doesn't it seem strange that there's…something that we never mention?

RACHEL. What?

SHEILA. The D word. We never mention it. The fact that I'm dying. Honey, we never talk about it.

RACHEL. I'm sorry, it's hard for me.

SHEILA. Well, I'm dying. And people who have faith die differently than people who don't have faith. I know it. I've seen it. And I don't want to be like them. So do me a favor, don't feel betrayed.

RACHEL. You can't tell me how to feel.

SHEILA. I just did.

RACHEL. Okay I won't.

SHEILA. Okay.

RACHEL. Maybe tomorrow when I come, we can go outside and smoke a bowl.

SHEILA. The family that gets high together, stays together, prays together.

RACHEL. I love you.

(She kisses SHEILA on the cheek.)

SHEILA. Love you, too.

RACHEL. *(Pause. RACHEL searching for a reason.)* Did I let you down?

SHEILA. Of course not.

RACHEL. But you feel empty.

SHEILA. This has nothing to do with you, I'd be proud of you no matter what you did.

RACHEL. Really

SHEILA. Yes.

RACHEL. Remember what I used to ask you when I was little?

(SHEILA shakes her head.)

I came home one day, I think I got in a fight with somebody in the schoolyard and I asked you, "Ma, would you still love me if I killed someone"?

SHEILA. What did I say?

RACHEL. You told me to wash my hands.

RACHEL. *(She moves to the door.)* Bye. I'll see you tomorrow.

SHEILA. Bye Sweetheart, drive carefully. Leave the door open I want to air this place out.

(RACHEL exits. SHEILA moves to the window, watching her walk across the parking lot. She reaches for the phone and begins dialing.)

SHEILA. Barbara Newman please. Oh, hi, Barbara, how are you? Good. Oh, you know, good days and bad. How is the paperwork coming along…the changes that I… Why not? Well, when will they be ready? Those changes have to be made by the end of the month. Okay. No – the end of the month. Right. So once everything is in order you can come by and I'll sign whatever and that'll be…

*(She sees, framed in the doorway, **DR. JULIUS STRONG**. He is a dashing black man in his early 50s. He wears a sharp suit and has a magnetic stare. His smile is constant, but not painted on. Despite the trappings of his profession, there is something endearing about his demeanor.)*

SHEILA. *(continued)* …that'll be that. Thanks for all your help Barbara. So long.

(Barbara hangs up the phone.)

JULIUS. Excuse me. Good afternoon.

SHEILA. Hello.

JULIUS. I'm sorry, I didn't mean to interrupt you. I'm looking for Sheila Gold.

SHEILA. That would be me.

JULIUS. I'm Dr. Julius Strong.

SHEILA. I know.

(Blackout)

Scene Two

(Later that afternoon, **SHEILA** *and* **JULIUS** *are laughing.)*

JULIUS. See sometimes you get what we call a "show me" congregation, you understand? They all sit back all fuss and frowns, arms folded back like this. *(He demonstrates).* And they're saying, "Uh-huh. Uh-huh. Okay Reverend, go ahead. You wanna take me to the Promised Land? All right. But you gotta show me some miracles first. Split the red sea. Turn some water into wine or something." But this group, no, no. They're up and yelling and I'm thinking, this is gonna be like shooting fish in a barrel. And I'm just about to quiet everybody down and start to speak, when I notice right there about ten feet above my head, circling like the Goodyear Blimp…is a fly. Not just any old fly. Like one of them big old horseflies. The kind that needs to register with the FAA. And it musta been a Baptist fly cause he's flying about like he's all excited speaking in tongues. And I kinda got my eye on him 'cause he seems to be a fly on a mission. So the music dies down and the crowd sits down and everybody's waiting on me. I open my mouth and give 'em a great big, "Good Morning and Glory Be to God Hallelujah." And right when I hit the "Uh" in "Hallelujah", wouldn't you know that fly just up and buzzed right inside my mouth.

SHEILA. Oh my God.

JULIUS. What could I do? They all answered back, "Halleluiah." And I just stood there and went like this.

(He nods up and down and demonstrates a kind of dance.)

Cause I don't know if I should swallow that there fly or spit him out or go get water or kneel down to pray, cause believe you me, there is nothing in the Preacher's Handbook about swallowing no Baptist Flies. And I can feel that horsefly flying around in there, trying to cut a new path to the afterlife. And everybody's looking at me and

I'm doing the horsefly dance, and wouldn't you know they all start doing the horsefly dance with me. And I got an entire congregation up on their feet wiggling up and down like we all trying to swallow that fly. And finally I just stopped and looked em up and down and I just let it out at the top of my lungs "PRAISE GOD" and that fly jumped out of my mouth faster than a sailor on a four hour pass. And he flew down the center aisle right out the double doors but wouldn't you know for the next hour, all those good folk kept dancing that Horsefly dance like it was a message from on high.

SHEILA. Did you tell them?

JULIUS. Me? No Sir! Don't kill the message or the messenger!

SHEILA. Now wait a minute, I've always wanted to ask you something.

JULIUS. Go ahead.

SHEILA. Okay. When you're moving up and down that stage and you hold the Bible open with one hand, how is it that you never lose your place?

JULIUS. Ah, now that's a trade secret.

SHEILA. What?

JULIUS. I couldn't.

SHEILA. Please.

JULIUS. You promise you'll never tell a soul?

SHEILA. I promise.

JULIUS. *(whispers)* Hair spray.

SHEILA. No.

JULIUS. From Leviticus to Deuteronomy, a little spritz around the edges and you will never be lost.

SHEILA. So that's it?

JULIUS. That's it. Oh, before I forget, I have a present for you.

(He reaches into a bag and pulls out a hardcover Bible.)

It's a New Testament, just like the ones you see on television, that we use at the ministry.

SHEILA. Thank you.

JULIUS. It is the book of Good News for all who come to his altar to receive.

SHEILA. Yes.

JULIUS. That's what gospel means, did you know that? Gospel means Good News.

SHEILA. I didn't know that.

JULIUS. Now, do you want me to get a little hair spray and spray the edges for you? That way, when you're at home running around this fine cottage, preaching the word of the lord along with Reverend Julius, you too can never lose your place!

(He does an imitation of himself preaching, **SHEILA** *laughs.)*

SHEILA. Oh, wait. I have something for you, too.

JULIUS. No.

SHEILA. It's just a little something. *I knew you were coming, I just didn't know when.* Here you are.

(She hands him a small box.)

JULIUS. You shouldn't have.

SHEILA. It's the least I could have done. Open it.

JULIUS. *(opening it)* It's a fountain pen.

SHEILA. The written word shapes the spoken word.

JULIUS. Oh my goodness –

SHEILA. Do you like it?

JULIUS. I love it. I haven't seen a pen like this in years.

SHEILA. You fill it up from the side.

JULIUS. Yes, yes. I know. This lever moves up, right?

SHEILA. And you draw the ink from the well.

JULIUS. It's beautiful. Very...what's the word...elegant.

SHEILA. I suppose.

JULIUS. It is. This is no pen to be writing out a shopping list. This is a pen to write a letter to a long lost friend, to someone in need, to a lover, so far away from you...

SHEILA. Yes.

JULIUS. *(He places his hand on top of hers.)* I shall treasure it always.

(She smiles. And the two catch eyes for a moment.)

All right. I'm not going to pull any punches now. There is another side to this visit of course.

(He takes his hand away.)

I read your last letter and I was truly touched. I am honored by the fact that you would even consider making such a generous contribution. It was totally unexpected. And I promise you, should you decide to follow through on this commitment –

SHEILA. Oh, I'm serious about it –

JULIUS. Well, I appreciate that. I'm here to assure you that it will be put to good use. The plans for the new campus are being finalized and we plan to begin building next fall. And your donation represents a giant leap in attaining our goals. Imagine the students and the good they will do in the world all because of your generosity. Praise God.

(pause)

Did you want to…make this a personal check or a banker's…uh, a certified….I'm sorry, how did you… what would be the best way for you to…

SHEILA. Well, I do have a lawyer who's handling my estate…

JULIUS. I see.

SHEILA. …and it's probably best to go through her.

JULIUS. Oh, I totally agree.

SHEILA. Because if there's one thing –

JULIUS. An amount this size –

SHEILA. – I've learned, it's –

JULIUS. – would certainly make a huge difference in our fundraising efforts. And it's important that everything is good and proper. Would it be easier for you if I was to contact her, or –

SHEILA. No, I don't think –

JULIUS. Just to reassure her that we are a legitimate church and that the money will go directly to the ministry and its work –

SHEILA. That won't be necessary.

JULIUS. It's just that if there are any questions –

SHEILA. Reverend –

JULIUS. Call me Julius.

SHEILA. Julius. That's a nice name.

JULIUS. I've always liked it. Liked saying it out loud, because you can play with the word so much. Like you're on a mountaintop. JUUUU – LEE – US. Or if you're in a tight spot, and you have to negotiate out of it, you take the quick attack. Jul-yus Strong, pleasure to meet you.

SHEILA. Or you can just sing it. Julius.

(She puts his name to a romantic tune, singing. He is a bit uncomfortable. Pause)

I've made arrangements for her to contact you. And I'm sure a check will go out by the end of the month.

JULIUS. I see.

SHEILA. Did you want it now?

JULIUS. What?

SHEILA. The check.

JULIUS. Oh no, not at all.

SHEILA. Well, you know what the cynical side of me would say.

JULIUS. I didn't know you had a cynical side.

(They both laugh.)

What would that side say?

SHEILA. Never mind.

JULIUS. You can tell me.

SHEILA. I wanted to meet you first.

JULIUS. I wanted to meet you, too.

SHEILA. I was always very careful with my money.

JULIUS. Of course. In this day and age, one can't be too careful.

SHEILA. I was a hard nosed businesswoman.

JULIUS. Oh, I can't imagine that.

SHEILA. I was. "Sheila's Closet" did millions in sales, we had 200 employees, believe me, you don't get to that level without stepping on a few toes

JULIUS. You seem so nice.

SHEILA. I have the soul of a banker but I wear the mask of a bohemian.

(They both laugh.)

Or maybe I wear the mask of a banker and the bohemian got drunk and left while I was counting my money. I don't know.

JULIUS. What about all your travels?

SHEILA. What?

JULIUS. You wrote to me, about taking trips to Nepal and India and doing Transcendental Meditation.

SHEILA. When did I….

JULIUS. Wait, I brought this one. Wait.

(He goes to his overcoat.)

SHEILA. What did you bring?

JULIUS. Your letter. This one.

(He pulls it out of the jacket pocket.)

SHEILA. Oh gosh –

JULIUS. This I think is my favorite.

(reading)

"I was searching for the kind of life I wish I had led. Where I felt everything was leading to something greater. Where I felt things deeply and saw the moon and stars and felt alive as much as I could. And where each day, I woke up and saw the possibility in things." That doesn't sound like the soul of a banker.

SHEILA. I wrote that?

JULIUS. Of course you did.

(laughing)

SHEILA. I was just trying to impress you.

JULIUS. No, it's more than that and you know it.

SHEILA. Well….

(She reaches into a drawer in her nightstand…)

I saved all of yours, too.

JULIUS. Really?

(pulling out a stack of letters)

SHEILA. Six months worth.

JULIUS. Wow. When did we start?

SHEILA. Um…I wrote you first and that was…September 14. So what's that, just over six months.

JULIUS. At least.

SHEILA. I was surprised when you wrote back.

JULIUS. Oh, I had to. I always looked forward to your letters. I would even re-read them once or twice, they're so wonderfully written.

SHEILA. Yours are.

JULIUS. Letter writing is a lost art, isn't it? I get hundreds of emails every day, but there's something wonderful about holding the written words of another in your hands. Feeling the space where they put pen to paper, where they spent a moment, and left part of themselves behind, to send a little smile your way.

SHEILA. Here's my favorite.

(reading.)

"I stood at the edge and I looked down. And I saw nothing. And I called out into the darkness because I couldn't stand to be so alone. And no echo came back to me. Only silence. But it was a true silence. The kind of silence where all I could hear was the beating of my own heart. And in that moment I came to enjoy the peace of being truly alone. For in that peace, there is love. And love is the only thing that matters.

JULIUS. That's nice.

SHEILA. It is.

SHEILA. Before I met you…before we started writing, I felt so empty. I had built all this from the ground up, I got on the cover of New York Business. People began calling me this tough bitch – excuse my French – when I knew deep down that I wasn't. I had made all this money and for what? So I went off looking for Mecca, thinking that maybe it would justify all the crummy things I did. And believe me, I did a lot of crummy things. And eventually I decided it was okay to be two people. To have one face that I showed the world but the real face, the real me, I would keep to myself and my family.

JULIUS. How did that work?

SHEILA. Not very well. Pretty crazy, huh? You spend your whole life looking for something, when deep down you know, that whatever it is, you're really not ready to find it. So I stopped looking.

JULIUS. But now you're ready to look again.

SHEILA. You know, I think I am.

JULIUS. Good.

SHEILA. It's funny, up until a year ago, I was an agnostic.

JULIUS. Oh. And are you still an agnostic?

SHEILA. There are no agnostics on cancer wards.

JULIUS. Yes.

(pause)

Well, anyway…I will wait for your lawyer to contact me.

SHEILA. This was all a total accident you know.

JULIUS. How's that?

SHEILA. I couldn't sleep and I was flicking around and I ran into your program and I began to watch and all of a sudden, I felt so alive. Like a huge burden had been lifted.

JULIUS. It was Christ speaking to you.

SHEILA. I thought I was dying. Well, I *know* I'm dying. But right then, I know it sounds corny, but it was as if my pain had been lifted. I felt light and I thought, well this must be it. This must be what it feels like. But then an hour later, I was still sitting here, still alive, still listening to you, hearing you speak, and I felt this rush of excitement –

JULIUS. Yes. Because you're on the verge of something great. You're about to enter another place, a better place.

SHEILA. Well, I don't know about that.

JULIUS. Come on now. This…

(He touches his chest.)

…is a useless cocoon. When we're ready, we cast it aside.

SHEILA. Look what's happened to my body. I used to play golf and tennis, I was in very good shape –

JULIUS. I can see.

SHEILA. I was. I spent hours in the gym, lot of good it did me, my husband left me for a younger woman –

JULIUS. Terrible.

SHEILA. Oh, this was years ago. I'm over it, she can have him.

JULIUS. It's a terrible thing to break up a family.

SHEILA. Well, yeah, but….well, you're right. My daughter was devastated and…how did I get on this?

JULIUS. Your excitement.

SHEILA. My excitement, yes. I based so much of what people thought of me on my appearance and in the long run, it did me no good. All the step classes in the world couldn't save my marriage. For that matter they couldn't make me happy. Or keep me healthy even.

JULIUS. It comes from within.

SHEILA. I knew that. I always knew that, but I think I must have thought it was something I would get to, you know

(pause)

Are you married?

JULIUS. No.

SHEILA. Have you ever been?

JULIUS. I was close once, but it just didn't seem right for me. Are you okay?

SHEILA. My stomach's a bit upset.

JULIUS. Oh, we don't have time for that.

SHEILA. No?

JULIUS. No, we don't. There's too much living to do. That's what's wrong with this place.

(He rises.)

It's full of a bunch of people sitting around waiting for something to happen. What is the point in that?

SHEILA. Yes.

JULIUS. God doesn't want that. God doesn't want us to lie around waiting for the resurrection.

(He takes her by the hand and pulls her out of bed.)

He wants us to be up and running and gasping and shouting and laughing and crying and living!

SHEILA. Oh my.

JULIUS. We need to brighten things up around here. Let's open the blinds...

...and bring in some fresh air and God's light and.... music!

SHEILA. Oh, there's a radio –

JULIUS. Where?

SHEILA. On the dresser –

JULIUS. It's perfect. Ah ha!

(He finds an up tempo Motown song on the radio)

This is what we need!

SHEILA. I like this...No, I don't dance...

JULIUS. Yes, you do!...

SHEILA. No...

JULIUS. Come on...

SHEILA. Oh, all right....

(He takes her by the hands and the two begin dancing.)

JULIUS. That's it now! *(He sings with the song.)* Sing it, sister.

SHEILA. I don't know the words.

JULIUS. Neither do I. Just fake it!

(JULIUS instructs her in the "pony.")

Stay with me now, stay with me...here it comes...

SHEILA. *(screams in joy, trying to keep up.)* Aah!

JULIUS. Pony with me, Pony with me!

SHEILA. I can't believe I'm doing this.

JULIUS. Come on, that's it.

(He kicks off his shoes, forces her to do the same and the two jump on top of the bed and finish their dance. The music stops and the two crash onto the bed.)

SHEILA. Oh my goodness.

JULIUS. That...is living.

(We hear another Motown song on the radio)

SHEILA. I'm exhausted.

JULIUS. Nonsense. You're alive.

SHEILA. It's so exciting to have you here.

JULIUS. Oh, please.

SHEILA. It is, I forgot I was sick.

JULIUS. Stop it, you're not sick. Not while Martha's playing, and especially not while I'm here. There is nothing greater than the healing power of music. And being in the word of the Lord.

SHEILA. And being with you.

(He smiles, embarrassed.)

It's true. It's your charisma.

JULIUS. I'm just a servant.

SHEILA. It's hard to stay positive.

JULIUS. Now, now –

SHEILA. I know, I know. Not as long as you're here.

JULIUS. No, not as long as *you're* here.

SHEILA. It was such a rush when I was first diagnosed. I mean, at first, it hit me like a ton of bricks; but once the initial shock was over, I was excited. Isn't that strange? As if I was looking forward to the challenge. I had just sold the business, Rachel was fine and I was on my own. And I thought, gosh, I'm going to go through this alone. And I told myself, well, it's okay, you were going stale anyway. Right? As if this was just something that came along to give me something to do, some kind of meaning. And I thought if anyone could do this, I could. I mean, hey, run a marathon, start a business, go through a divorce, raise a family, no problem. Cancer? Sure next case. What in the world was I thinking?

JULIUS. You're a strong woman.

SHEILA. Until I started chemo.

JULIUS. Ah.

SHEILA. A steady diet of High Test is a real eye opener, let me tell you. But even then, I kept thinking, oh the next MRI will show some progress, or one of these cocktails is sure to work. And then one day I found myself here. And it's very difficult. My daughter comes to visit and she's full of pep talks. She brings me…marijuana to smoke because it helps my appetite and the nausea.

JULIUS. I was wondering what that smell was.

SHEILA. Yeah, you must have thought I was some kind of junkie.

JULIUS. No, I've heard that it helps.

SHEILA. But I don't know what I would have done if I hadn't begun watching you. It's as if you've opened a whole other world to me.

(He takes her hands.)

JULIUS. Sheila, are you ready to accept Christ as your savior?

SHEILA. I don't know.

JULIUS. His love for you knows no bounds.

SHEILA. I think it has more to do with you.

(*pause*)

I know you came all this way and I love listening to you speak but...I can't imagine myself being anything but a Jew.

JULIUS. As was true for Saint Paul. He never met Christ, never met the Apostles, never saw himself as anything but a Jew. But one day God revealed himself to Paul. "I neither received it of man, neither was I taught it, but by the revelation of Jesus Christ."

SHEILA. I'm also pro-choice.

JULIUS. Hmm.

SHEILA. I've always been pro-choice.

JULIUS. I understand, that's a complicated issue.

SHEILA. Yeah, but...you're not. Right? You're pro-life.

JULIUS. At the Heritage Ministries, we try not to focus on the negative. If a woman is in a situation where she has a baby that she cannot imagine keeping, then it's our job to find a way to bring that baby into the world and find the child a home. We like to say we're pro-choice too and we choose life. Always focus on the positive. Let's not dwell on the past and what was done. Let's look ahead to the place...we're trying to get to.

(*The two share a look. There's an uncomfortable pause.*)

Shall we pray for guidance?

SHEILA. Why not.

(*He folds his hands, but she then reaches out and unfolds them. Taking one hand in each of hers.* **JULIUS** *smiles and then closes his eyes intently.* **SHEILA** *looks first to the hands and then to* **JULIUS**, *eyes wide open.*)

JULIUS. Let us pray.

(*pause*)

Dear Lord, we humbly ask your blessing in the name of Jesus Christ. We pray to thee –

SHEILA. Wait.

(JULIUS *opens his eyes.*)

JULIUS. What is it?

SHEILA. I don't think I can do this.

JULIUS. (JULIUS *takes her hands again.*) What do you want from Christ?

SHEILA. He's taking requests?

JULIUS. All the time. Put your life in his hands. Are you ready to be born again? Sheila, are you ready to accept him as your lord and savior?

SHEILA. That, I really don't know.

JULIUS. He's there for you always. "Death is swallowed up in victory. Death, where is your sting? The sting of death is sin and the power of sin is the law; but thanks be to God who gives us the victory through our Messiah, Jesus."

SHEILA. You're always on.

JULIUS. What do you mean?

SHEILA. I mean you're always on.

JULIUS. I don't understand.

SHEILA. You don't have to always be that way.

JULIUS. What way?

SHEILA. You don't have to always be in…preacher mode. I know, it's what you do and you're a showman in some way, but sometimes I would read your letters and they didn't sound like you.

JULIUS. Of course they did. I wrote them.

SHEILA. But there was something different. You seem a lot…I can't say this.

JULIUS. What?

SHEILA. You're a lot more than the person we see on television.

JULIUS. Well, everyone has different sides that…you said yourself –

SHEILA. Wait, wait.

(*She pulls out a letter and begins to read.*)

SHEILA. *(cont.)* "How is it that the all knowing God calls out to Adam, 'where art thou?' But it's not a literal question. It's the question God calls out to everyone. Where are you in your world? So many years and days of those allotted to you have passed, and how far have you gotten?"

JULIUS. I didn't write that. That's Martin Buber.

SHEILA. I know of very few evangelicals who quote Martin Buber.

JULIUS. You know of very few evangelicals.

SHEILA. You're smarter than them. You're smarter than that television persona.

(pause)

I'm sorry. I shouldn't have said that.

JULIUS. No…its…

SHEILA. Maybe this wasn't the best idea.

JULIUS. …quite all right.

SHEILA. I appreciate you coming all this way, but –

JULIUS. No, no. That's a good question. Where are you? I often ask myself the same thing. Where have I gone? I feel as though I haven't gotten anywhere. Where am I?

SHEILA. You're here.

JULIUS. I believe that everything happens for a reason. I believe the Lord brought us together.

SHEILA. You really think that?

JULIUS. He loves your very soul. The living God wants to temple in thee. Ask of him, that he may enter your soul. Ask of him, that he may plant his seed in your fertile and loving heart.

SHEILA. See, you're doing it again.

JULIUS. Of course. It's what I do, it's who I am.

SHEILA. Really?

JULIUS. I'm a preacher. I'm Dr. Julius Strong.

SHEILA. I know.

(Pause. They share a look.)

SHEILA. I'm sorry. I think its best if you –

JULIUS. Don't be afraid. Ask of him.

SHEILA. I can't.

JULIUS. He's always there for you.

SHEILA. I don't want anything of him. How can I start praying to a God I abandoned years ago?

JULIUS. People do it all the time.

SHEILA. People can be pretty foolish.

JULIUS. He's always ready to forgive and welcome you home.

SHEILA. Maybe I'm not ready to forgive. Maybe he abandoned me.

JULIUS. If you're turning your back on God, you're saying he does exist.

SHEILA. Fine. He exists. And I have nothing to ask of him.

JULIUS. Then ask it of me.

SHEILA. Ask what?

JULIUS. Whatever you need. Ask it of me. I'm here for you.

SHEILA. You are.

JULIUS. Yes.

SHEILA. Do you mean that?

JULIUS. Yes.

SHEILA. *(Pause. And then quietly.)* Hold me.

JULIUS. What?

SHEILA. Come here and hold me.

JULIUS. I'm not –

SHEILA. Just do it.

*(After an awkward moment, **JULIUS** moves to the bedside. He sits next to **SHEILA** on the upper half of the bed, looking out, his arms around her. She lays her head on his chest. After a moment, **JULIUS** begins to stroke her hair.)*

SHEILA. Do you like my wig?

JULIUS. It feels real.

SHEILA. It is. 2000 dollars, all the human hair money can buy. I hate it.

JULIUS. It looks good on you. Does someone style it?

> (**SHEILA** *takes his hand off of her head. She moves it to her mouth and kisses it.* **JULIUS** *stands there, frozen. The two kiss. And then* **JULIUS** *pulls away. He sits on the bed, but does not face her. He looks at the wall, seemingly in shock.*)

I'm sorry, I shouldn't have done that.

SHEILA. You didn't do anything.

JULIUS. What am I...doing...

SHEILA. I'll shut the blinds now, I want to sleep.

> (**JULIUS** *reaches over and draws the blinds. He lingers at the window for a bit.*)

What are you doing?

JULIUS. It's gotten dark so quickly.

SHEILA. Sometimes I sleep with the light on. Just something about the darkness and listening to the sound of...I don't know, nothing I supposed. That's when you truly understand how relentless the time is. The time alone and the silence. Sometimes I just lie here and talk out loud to God. Or to no one, I don't know.

JULIUS. God hears you.

SHEILA. Does he?

JULIUS. Of course. Every word, every thought, every prayer –

SHEILA. Well, even if he doesn't, it's good to say things out loud.

JULIUS. It's good to know the sound of your own voice. Maybe that's something you can only get in the darkness.

SHEILA. Come here and hold me.

> (**JULIUS** *moves to the side of the bed.*)

JULIUS. I'm not –

SHEILA. Please.

(After an awkward moment, **JULIUS** *moves to the bedside. He sits next to* **SHEILA** *on the upper half of the bed, looking out, his arms around her. She lays her head on his chest.)*

JULIUS. I can see you in the moonlight.

*(***JULIUS** *begins to stroke her hair.)*

SHEILA. Do that.

(She grimaces.)

JULIUS. Are you all right?

SHEILA. It hurts.

JULIUS. Should I call someone?

SHEILA. No, it'll pass. I want you to take off your clothes and get under the covers with me.

JULIUS. I….

SHEILA. Please.

(After a moment, **JULIUS** *stands. He kicks off his shoes, takes off his jacket, loosens his tie, and gets under the covers with* **SHEILA**. *She turns so that her head rests on his chest.* **JULIUS** *holds her and strokes her hair, but looks uncomfortable.)*

Tell me a story. Tell me a story like you do on television.

JULIUS. *(pause)* Our Savior instructed the apostles to take him to the desolate shores of Gennesaret. He had been preaching all day and wanted a quiet place to rest. They took the boat into deeper waters as the lord lay down at the front of the boat, fast asleep. No sooner had they cast their nets, when the skies turned dark fierce winds began to blow and a tempest rocked the boat. They called to Jesus, but he was fast asleep. They yelled and shook him, with all their might and fear, but still he did not wake. Finally, they cried out, "Lord save us, we perish." At this cry, the Lord awoke and laying his hands over the sea, he says quietly, "Peace, be still." And clouds rolled away, the winds died down, and the tempest was quieted.

*(**SHEILA** reaches her hand up and pulls **JULIUS** lips to hers. Pulling his head down to hers, she kisses him passionately. Lights fade to black.)*

End Act One

ACT 2

Scene One

(Setting is the same as the top of the play. It is early Sunday morning. The sun shines through the open window. **SHEILA** *lies in bed asleep. Her wig is off and her hair is quite short.* **JULIUS** *sits naked on a chair at the foot of the bed facing her. After a moment* **SHEILA** *wakes up and the two look at one another for a moment.)*

JULIUS. Good morning.

SHEILA. Good morning.

JULIUS. How did you sleep?

SHEILA. Good. What time is it?

JULIUS. Eight.

SHEILA. There is a naked black man sitting next to me.

JULIUS. This is true. Should I get dressed?

SHEILA. Not unless you want to. Of course, if my daughter walked in right now, she would have a heart attack.

JULIUS. Yes. Maybe she would think I was the Angel of Mercy, come to take you home. Oh, excuse me miss. I won't be but a minute. What's that? Well, I don't know what version of the Bible you've been reading, but in our version, all the angels are quite naked.

SHEILA. How did you sleep?

JULIUS. Very well, thank you. I was watching you sleep and I wanted so much to just touch your face, but I was afraid I would wake you. And then I had a thought and I almost laughed out loud.

SHEILA. What?

JULIUS. Last night, did I make love to the bohemian or the banker?

SHEILA. I'll never tell.

JULIUS. Well, personally, I think it was the bohemian. The banker's been holding her place for a while, but the bohemian is getting ready to come back.

(They kiss.)

You were talking in your sleep.

SHEILA. I have a recurring dream. I'm in a plane and it's an old plane. Silvery. Like it hasn't been painted, just the exposed metal. We're flying over the Pacific Ocean and the light outside the plane is so intense, you have to squint. And there's no one in the plane. I'm sitting on the passenger side and I look over and Amelia Earhardt is driving the plane. And I'm about to ask her something when she looks over at me and just smiles. And I think, okay. I'll just look straight ahead and let her drive the plane. What do you suppose that means?

JULIUS. Well…you're traveling, you're on a journey. And you're willing to let go. And let someone else do the driving.

SHEILA. It doesn't mean that. You think it means that?

JULIUS. Van Gogh said, "Death will be our ferry to another star." Nice image, don't you think? It just means that this is all transitory.

SHEILA. I always wanted to meet Amelia Earhardt. When I was little, my mother would talk about her so much and I would read about all her flights and where she might have ended up. I thought, if I die and go to heaven I'd like to meet her. If nothing else to find out what the hell happened.

JULIUS. You admire her.

SHEILA. So independent; didn't need any men around. Lived on her own terms, died on her own terms. Do you figure I'll get to see her?

JULIUS. Amelia? I'll put in a call and see what I can do.

SHEILA. I'm serious.

JULIUS. Can I borrow your toothbrush?

SHEILA. Go ahead.

(**JULIUS** *exits to the bathroom,* **SHEILA** *begins to put on her wig.*)

What do you think heaven is like?

JULIUS. *(O.S.)* I don't know. You tell me.

(We hear him brushing his teeth.)

SHEILA. You're the expert.

JULIUS. *(O.S.)* Since when?

SHEILA. Oh, come on. Your show, it's full of everybody dancing and singing about how great it is after and everlasting life and how all this is transitory.

(poking his head out)

JULIUS. Okay. Judaism is focused on the law. Right?

SHEILA. Yes.

JULIUS. So what does that tell you?

SHEILA. Its main focus is how to live your life here.

JULIUS. Yes. But also that there is a religious progression. We can say, perhaps, that each religion is a manifestation of the same deity. But that religions change to suit the needs of humanity. Pagan rituals existed at a time when primitive man was trying to understand the mystery of…what…the rising and falling of the sun, the cycle of the moon. In Judaism, many contributions. It gives the world monotheism, the law, the Talmud, it gives us the basis for Christianity. Christianity, the next step in the progression. Jesus, the Messiah, answers those questions left unaddressed by Judaism. This is why John 3:16 is so essential. The notion of everlasting life.

SHEILA. But can I change my religion just to suit my needs at a particular point in life?

JULIUS. Of course. People do it all the time.

SHEILA. Okay, so what is heaven.

JULIUS. You go first.

SHEILA. Why me?

JULIUS. Because I don't think you'll like my answer.

SHEILA. Well, I've thought about this. I had the notion that there might be a great deal to look forward to. That I would see people I hadn't seen before, that I would get to meet all these great historical figures, like Amelia and President Roosevelt. And my mother, I would get to see my mother and father, my Uncle Mike. That's my mother's brother. But then I began to wonder, how would I see them? Would I see them as I remembered them before they died? That doesn't make sense, why would there be an afterlife where people were existing at their weakest? Even though that might mean a great deal to me, that couldn't be any fun for them. And then I figured that maybe in heaven, you return to the age where you had the most fun. Or the age where you were most comfortable, like six years old or something. But if my mother was six years old, how in the world would I recognize her?

JULIUS. *(O.S.)* It almost seems a little…immature, isn't it?

SHEILA. How's that?

JULIUS. *(O.S.)* It's an immature idea to think that everything will last forever. Little children think that way. Dogs do. You leave the house in the morning, they bark like crazy as if you're never coming back. Things are supposed to end.

SHEILA. But your entire religion is based on the afterlife-

(**JULIUS** *appears from the bathroom, naked and brushing his teeth. He speaks garbled through the toothpaste.*)

JULIUS. I believe in the afterlife. I believe there is something called heaven, but I don't think it's anything like our present. There is a part of all of us that is eternal. And death means reuniting with that part. That's as simple as I can put it.

SHEILA. Oh come on, you can do better than that.

JULIUS. I told you, you wouldn't like my answer.

SHEILA. But you're supposed to know.

JULIUS. No, I'm supposed to make you *believe* that I know. And if I believe it strongly enough; I'll make you believe that you know. And once we believe there is a God, he exists.

SHEILA. How is that –

JULIUS. I'm in the business of helping you believe. And the best way to do that is to pretend that I know. Of course that wouldn't play very well on television, would it?

SHEILA. So, it's just a bunch of stories.

JULIUS. Yeah. But they're really good ones.

(Pause. **SHEILA** *smiles.)*

When I first began preaching and I had a small congregation in Wingrove, near where I grew up, Faith Evangelical Ministries and I was so proud and so happy because this is what I had always wanted. All I wanted was to be alone with my thoughts and prayers and meditation. I would have this little congregation and it would grow and I would be happy and that would be that. But nobody came. Not enough people to make a living at it anyway.

SHEILA. Why didn't anyone come?

JULIUS. I wasn't any good. I was confused and it showed and no one came. Because no one is going to get up on a Sunday morning and put on their best clothes to see you meditate and be all inside yourself, full of your own doubts and limitation. So I did a U Turn and changed my style. If people wanted big and brassy and over the top; well I could do that; I created a new persona, Dr. Julius Strong. A person born of faith; of the rock that is my belief in Jesus Christ, a man so certain that there is one way to heaven, one way to the living God. And I found out the bigger I got on the outside, the bigger I got on the inside. And the ministry grew from there and now we're coast to coast.

(Pause. He then sits back and speaks almost in a whisper.)

JULIUS. *(cont.)* Bigger than life. Bigger than life itself, this man. I look back at where I started, at that small preacher of a man, that boy from West Virginia…if he saw me today, he wouldn't even recognize what I've become.

SHEILA. And what have you become?

JULIUS. Good question. I wanted to be a different person. I wanted to be Thomas Merton and I ended up being Jimmy Swaggert.

SHEILA. Oh come on, that's not true.

JULIUS. The world is slippery grey. People want an answer. They want to know that somebody is out there that loves them. They want to believe that there's something after this. They want to believe they'll be saved at the end of it all.

(pause)

I learned a long time ago, you have to give the people what they need. And what they need is Dr. Julius Strong, Preacher, extraordinaire.

SHEILA. That's you.

JULIUS. That's me. Give me a topic, I'll testify.

SHEILA. Oh come on –

JULIUS. Go ahead, anything.

SHEILA. Oh, I don't know , water pitcher…no…fast food… umm, I know – McDonald's food.

JULIUS. McDonald's Food.

(He stands on the chair and grabs a Bible.)

I was standing in line, waiting on the line, like so many others, just waiting to be served, waiting to be nourished, waiting to place an order so my soul would be fulfilled. And I said, I would like to order some chicken McNuggets, please. Now, I didn't say I wanted to order any four piece. No, no, no. I said, I'd like the six piece; with some extra dipping sauce. Because I deserve it, don't you know. And I took my paper bag, and I was ready to accept the good grace of the Lord, and accept these six…nuggets of…what part of the chicken they are, I do not know. But there they were, just waiting for me and I sat down and just like that I realized I was lost, brothers and sisters. For I realized in my haste, I had forgotten to take myself some extra dipping sauce. I had no honey mustard. I had no spicy barbecue. It was nowhere to be found. I was at wit's end, the end of my rope. I would have to somehow manage with these poor, lonely, six chicken McNuggets, without a dipping sauce to dip them in. I was just about to give up, when sitting there on the bench, the McDonald Land bench, all alone, just me and my happy meal, I looked inside the bag, and there it was, sitting in the corner, like hope at the bottom of Pandora's box, one genuine container of dipping sauce. My searching was over. It was always there, brothers and sisters. Down in the very bottom of the bag they call life. Don't be searching for happiness, let happiness come to you. And remember to ask the girl for the sauce before you leave the counter. Praise God.

SHEILA. You make me forget I'm sick.

JULIUS. You make me feel so alive. I came here to give to you and it is you who are giving to me.

SHEILA. Do you?

JULIUS. What?

SHEILA. Need me?

JULIUS. *(He nods.)* We're cut from the same cloth, you and I. You know what it's like to show one face to the world and another to yourself.

SHEILA. Putting on a face to meet the faces that we meet.

JULIUS. Yes. It's so good to talk about these things.

SHEILA. But I'm dying.

JULIUS. Who isn't? Do you know what the French call it when you climax?

(She shakes her head.)

JULIUS. Le Petite Morte.

SHEILA. The little death.

JULIUS. That's right. When you're close to death, that's when you feel most alive. And it doesn't matter when it ends. As long as you keep on living till it does.

SHEILA. What could I possibly give to you?

JULIUS. I'm lonely. And I think your letters made me realize it. And then seeing you and being here…I had forgotten what that felt like.

SHEILA. I should be saying that to you. Wait a minute. Shouldn't you be in church?

JULIUS. Oh, I planned this trip for a while, there's someone covering for me. I was hoping that we could find some time to pray together later.

SHEILA. Sure, why not. *(pause)* I hate Sundays.

JULIUS. It's the Lord's Day.

SHEILA. Around here it's visiting day.

JULIUS. Doesn't your family come by?

SHEILA. They do. My daughter will be here soon, you'll get to meet her.

JULIUS. Oh?

SHEILA. She's a piece of work. She comes by, brings me a new stash of weed to get me through. And my ex-husband, Lenny, he used to come visit, but then he stopped.

(Pause. **SHEILA** *looks out the window.)*

Visiting day. You sit and you see families walking. And they're smiling and laughing and everybody's on their best behavior. If you didn't know any better, you'd never know there was anything wrong. And if you listen to their conversations, you know what people are saying? Nothing. They're not saying anything. You'd think everybody would be in some kind of a hurry to talk about…I don't know, things left undone, or unsaid. I loved our times together, or I don't regret marrying you, or I never liked your noodle kugel, or it always bothered me when you wore your hair that way. I cheated on you once on a business trip. I don't know why, I just did. Think about me when I'm gone. But they don't. No one says anything of any significance. No one mentions the word death. It's almost as if there's a man behind the curtain and he's going to come out and say, Okay, game's up. You can go home now. You passed the test. Whatever. And then everyone goes home and the night falls and this place gets real quiet. And it begins to smell like death again.

(pause)

I think I need to smoke.

(JULIUS goes to get his coat.)

Where are you going?

JULIUS. I thought I would get some breakfast for the two of us.

SHEILA. Oh, you don't have to do that.

JULIUS. No, I want to. You can spark a J and I'll get us some Chinese food.

SHEILA. Chinese food?

JULIUS. Sure. Will you have some?

SHEILA. Where are you gonna get Chinese at nine o'clock in the morning?

JULIUS. I have my ways.

SHEILA. Wait, wait. You can't have Chinese for breakfast.

JULIUS. Why not?

SHEILA. Because it's not breakfast food.

JULIUS. Don't they eat breakfast in China?

SHEILA. Yes, but –

JULIUS. Every now and then, you gotta do something crazy. Just to remind yourself that you're still alive.

(He kisses her.)

I'll get the food and when I come back, we'll eat our Chinese breakfast. And then, well...

SHEILA. What?

JULIUS. I have to ask you something.

SHEILA. What is it?

JULIUS. I don't want you to think this is too forward of me, but, I'd very much like it if you moved to Heritage Creek. To live with me.

SHEILA. Are you serious?

JULIUS. Yes. We can be closer together, the church can pay for your move –

SHEILA. But what about Rachel?

JULIUS. If Rachel wants so badly to visit you, she can come to California then, can't she?

SHEILA. I can't just leave –

JULIUS. Why not? Just think about it. You don't have to decide today.

SHEILA. I don't have much time left.

JULIUS. You have to stop thinking that way. You are very much alive. That's the problem with these places. It's full of people who have given up. What could be worse for the soul than a room full of those without hope in Christ? I'm here to tell you the Good News that is our Gospel. That there is always hope. Because where there is hope, there is faith. And where there is faith, there is God. Your will is strong, your faith is getting stronger, you need to be with others who believe.

SHEILA. You're doing it again.

JULIUS *(laughs)* I am.

(pause)

You need to be with me. I need you.

(They kiss.)

SHEILA. Okay wait, I have to ask you something.

JULIUS. Go ahead.

SHEILA. It's silly.

JULIUS. Just ask.

SHEILA. Is this about us? Or is it about God?

JULIUS. It's about both. I look at you and I see the beauty of God's light. Right there, right in front of me, like manna from the heavens.

SHEILA. What do I do with you?

JULIUS. Have a little faith.

(They kiss.)

SHEILA. What are you –

JULIUS. A little faith.

(They kiss.)

Just a little.

(They kiss again.)

In me.

(He exits.)

SHEILA. *(quietly)* In me.

(Blackout)

Scene Two

(An hour later. **SHEILA** *lies in bed, holding a smoldering pipe.* **RACHEL** *enters. She looks around the room, thinking to straighten things out a bit. Then she notices the pipe burning. She removes it from her hand and sits next to her mother, watching her as she sleeps.)*

SHEILA. Shh.

(still sleeping.)

RACHEL. It's okay, Ma.

SHEILA. Okay.

RACHEL. Go to sleep.

SHEILA. Okay.

(pause)

Who's that?

RACHEL. It's me, Ma.

SHEILA. *(opening her eyes)* Who?

RACHEL. Hi.

SHEILA. Oh.

(She sits up suddenly.)

RACHEL. It's okay. Sleep.

SHEILA. No. I was surprised.

RACHEL. That you woke up?

SHEILA. I'm always surprised when I wake up.

(She begins looking around the room.)

What time is it?

RACHEL. A little after 10. Did you call and order breakfast? It's late.

SHEILA. Oh, yeah. I was um....I didn't feel like eating.

RACHEL. Oh. Do you want something now?

SHEILA. I don't know.

RACHEL. How much did you smoke?

SHEILA. I don't know. I fell asleep.

RACHEL. You gotta be careful, you could burn the place down. Let me get some sun in here.

(She goes to the window and opens the shade, etc. .)

So guess who I saw last night?

SHEILA. Who?

RACHEL. Barbara Newman.

SHEILA. Oh? How is she?

RACHEL. Good. We went out to Bogarts for drinks. She's all excited, she's going on vacation.

SHEILA. Where's she going?

RACHEL. Bahamas. She's got one of those packages, a four-day deal. She's flying out tonight.

SHEILA. Good for her. You ought to do something like that.

RACHEL. Barbara said that you've been calling the office a lot.

SHEILA. So?

RACHEL. Is there something you'd like to tell me?

SHEILA. No.

RACHEL. Okay.

SHEILA. I thought I was allowed to have a private conversation with my lawyer.

*(**SHEILA** rises, puts on her shoes, etc.)*

RACHEL. You are. I just wondered what you were doing, that's all.

SHEILA. It's none of your business.

RACHEL. You're right, it isn't. I'm a little surprised you would keep something from me –

SHEILA. I'm not keeping –

RACHEL. But then again, I guess I shouldn't be, the way you've been acting.

SHEILA. – anything from you. For God's sake –

RACHEL. I mean, I know you're not feeling well, I just didn't think you would go behind my back –

SHEILA. Am I your daughter now?

RACHEL. – and change things after we worked so hard to set things in order.

SHEILA. Because I would have thought – oh "we" worked so hard? Since when did "we" work together on anything?

RACHEL. I was the one who found you this lawyer.

SHEILA. What are you talking about? I had a lawyer. I was doing your friend a favor by hiring her.

RACHEL. I mean a real lawyer, Barbara knows about these things.

SHEILA. Apparently not, because she doesn't know enough to keep her mouth shut.

RACHEL. It's her job to advise you when she thinks you're about to do something foolish.

SHEILA. Like what?

RACHEL. You tell me.

SHEILA. I don't know what you're talking about.

RACHEL. Barbara told me you were considering making a major withdrawal out of your account.

SHEILA. Remind me to fire her ass.

RACHEL. I'm just amazed at your lack of trust. Like, since when do you keep all this from me?

SHEILA. Since when do you care?

RACHEL. I care. What's the matter with you. Of course, I care! What makes you think I don't?

SHEILA. I'm amazed that you could be so insulting to me.

RACHEL. Barbara just –

SHEILA. – that you would stoop so low to ask your friend to spy on me.

RACHEL. She just thought it was unusual, that's all.

SHEILA. Well, it's none of her business and it's none of yours.

RACHEL. Okay fine. If that's what you want to do, go ahead.

SHEILA. I will.

(pause)

RACHEL. I brought you some more muffins.

SHEILA. I don't want a muffin. I'm having –

RACHEL. Eat some of this, it's bran.

SHEILA. I don't want a goddamned bran muffin! That's all you do is bring me food. Oh excuse me, first you bring me the weed so I can eat the food. And then the cleaning lady comes in to eat the food that I leave behind. Why the hell does anybody even bother? You've decided that it's time to treat me like some kind of a child, incapable of making my own decisions. Someone whose face needs stuffing and whose ass needs wiping. Well guess what, I'm not ready to play that role, all right? So stop acting like little miss Florence Nightingale and treat me like an adult.

RACHEL. *(quietly, shocked)* Okay.

SHEILA. I'm not ready for it.

RACHEL. I heard you the first time.

SHEILA. All right. Go to the store and get me some orange juice. Please.

RACHEL. Fine.

(She moves to the door.)

You know that preacher you listen to is broke.

SHEILA. Who?

RACHEL. You know who I mean. Julius Strong. He's way over his head in debt, he's trying to float a bond. Looks to me like he's running that church of his into the ground.

SHEILA. Well, he's building a university and he has a major real estate expansion planned. And that does cost a lot of money.

RACHEL. Mom, he is broke. Get it?

SHEILA. I don't want to talk about this.

RACHEL. Yeah, that's the problem. I wish you had discussed with me before you –

SHEILA. I need some seltzer, too.

RACHEL. Fine. This guy is nothing but a walking Ponzi Scheme.

(SHEILA *turns her head away from* **RACHEL** *and faces the window.* **RACHEL** *moves to the door and practically bumps into* **JULIUS STRONG**, *entering with Chinese food.*)

JULIUS. Oh, hello. You must be Rachel.

SHEILA. Julius, this is my daughter.

JULIUS. I've heard so much about you.

RACHEL. You're the guy on TV.

JULIUS. Uh, yes. I suppose. Pleased to meet you.

RACHEL. What are you doing here?

JULIUS. I came to visit your mother.

(*He begins to put down the food.*)

All right now. It was a little early, so I could only get some vegetarian dishes. We have broccoli in garlic sauce…this is an eggplant dish…

RACHEL. Wait. For breakfast?

SHEILA. Sure. Why not?

RACHEL. Where did you get this?

JULIUS. I happened to notice on the way in that this place, Kam Wei kitchen is open all night. Apparently he has a bunch of truck drivers who stop during the night, so I figured he would be open and we'd have Chinese for breakfast and –

(*to* **RACHEL**)

Will you be joining us?

RACHEL. No. I've got muffins.

JULIUS. Suit yourself.

RACHEL. How did you get here?

JULIUS. I flew in from California yesterday. Didn't your mother tell you?

(*She shakes her head, no.*)

She's been writing me for quite a while and I was so moved by her letters that I knew I had to pay her a visit.

RACHEL. You still want juice?

SHEILA. No, forget it. Mmm, that's good.

JULIUS. Would you like an egg roll?

SHEILA. Oh, I love egg rolls.

JULIUS. Coming right up.

(He gives one to SHEILA.)

Rachel?

RACHEL. No thank you.

(JULIUS and SHEILA eat. RACHEL watches them giggle, etc.)

JULIUS. Your mother has told me so much about you.

RACHEL. I'll bet.

JULIUS. You've done a great job taking care of her. I know how difficult it must be, working as you do, and taking care of someone.

RACHEL. Well, I –

JULIUS. Sheila was talking about all the pot runs you do for her. That must be an amazing task, week after week, isn't it?

RACHEL. You go to the park, you can usually score.

JULIUS. I suppose.

SHEILA. This is very good.

JULIUS. Many years ago, I lived in Chicago and my neighborhood had all sorts of drug trafficking. And the drug dealers in the neighborhood had this elaborate system, every corner was watched and every corner had a signal. They could be selling all sorts of things one minute, but if a patrol car was coming through, one guy would throw his hat in the air or rub his nose, and they'd all scatter and be gone in five seconds. I used to think, if these police would just drive in and out of the neighborhood like a dozen times an hour, they'd exhaust the heck out of these people and they'd just leave.

(He and **SHEILA** *laugh,* **RACHEL** *smiles.)*

JULIUS. *(cont.)* Now, you're the one who works at Planned Parenthood, is that correct?

RACHEL. That's right.

JULIUS. Wonderful organization. My brother James is a missionary in Nairobi. And he always talks of the fine work Planned Parenthood does there. Have you ever worked overseas?

RACHEL. No.

JULIUS. Ah, you should some time. It's an eye opening experience working in the Third World

RACHEL. Well, we've got our own problems in this one.

JULIUS. *(laughing)* Yes, I suppose.

(to **SHEILA***)*

How is that?

SHEILA. Delicious.

JULIUS. *(to* **RACHEL***)* Now, are you like me? Do you spend all your time here trying to get this young lady to eat something?

RACHEL. She never eats. Not like this.

JULIUS. I know. And you know what happens, you end up eating it yourself, right?

SHEILA. I'm eating, I'm eating.

JULIUS. Well, you keep on eating, otherwise we'll have to get you high again?

RACHEL. Do you?

JULIUS. What?

RACHEL. Get high?

JULIUS. Oh no. I have to say, I never understood what the big fuss was about. I tried some when I was a young man, this is back when I lived in West Virginia. It only made me tired. And if I wanted to be tired I could have gone to work in the mines like my Daddy and got high on the coal dust. And they woulda paid me to do that.

RACHEL. You've certainly been around.

JULIUS. I guess I have.

RACHEL. This was a pretty long trip.

JULIUS. To here? Oh, not really. I fly all the time. We have ministries all over the world. And we're on a bit of a break from the television show. They're running repeats.

RACHEL. Uh-huh. Do you visit everyone who writes you a letter?

JULIUS. I would if I could. I get so many requests for appearances, I barely have enough time to run the ministry.

RACHEL. It must take a lot of work to keep up that palace.

JULIUS. I would hardly call it a palace.

RACHEL. No, I saw the brochure. Where is that thing you had, Ma?

SHEILA. I don't know, it's here someplace.

RACHEL. I saw the plans though, it's very impressive. You're building a Bible college of some kind?

JULIUS. That's right. The plan is to have it completed in 2010, and it will be an accredited university – we actually could enroll a freshman class right now. We've had over 200 applicants and we've toyed with the idea of beginning things early.

RACHEL. So all this development you're doing, how much is this gonna cost?

JULIUS. Well, there's –

RACHEL. I mean I read something about how you're trying to raise $25 million over the next –

JULIUS. We've raised most of it already.

RACHEL. Really? That's great. How much more do you need?

JULIUS. Were you planning on making a donation?

RACHEL. No, but my mother is.

SHEILA. All right, Rachel. That's enough.

RACHEL. I guess I'm just curious, do you fly to the bedside of every sick patient who writes you, or just the ones who have fat checkbooks?

SHEILA. Rachel –

JULIUS. Your mother is at the end of one part of her life and at the beginning of another. She asked me to come to her to help her make that transition.

RACHEL. To what?

JULIUS. To heaven, to the afterlife.

RACHEL. You really think that's true?

JULIUS. It's true for those who have faith. It's true for those who are born again and have accepted Christ as their savior.

RACHEL. And it's especially true for those who give a fortune to whacko Evangelists.

SHEILA. I'm afraid I have to ask you to leave.

RACHEL. Me?

SHEILA. Yes you. You're insulting my friend –

RACHEL. I'm not insulting anyone. This is called –

JULIUS. Sheila, that's quite all right –

RACHEL *(overlapping)* – having a conversation.

JULIUS. I understand Rachel has some concerns.

RACHEL. You're damn right I do.

SHEILA. I would rather that you left.

RACHEL. So this is the thanks I get? For all the times I took time out of work to visit you and clean you up and make sure this place was –

SHEILA. Get out.

RACHEL. You can't do this. You can't just change everything like this. You can't turn your back on your own family and start believing in something that isn't true. This is a lie you told me not to believe and now you're gonna tell me, "Oh, never mind, I never meant that anyway, believe whatever you want."

SHEILA. And I'm not allowed to change my mind?

RACHEL. No, you're not. Just because you're dying that doesn't give you the right to change your mind.

SHEILA. I can't do this. I'm leaving.

RACHEL. Where are you going?

SHEILA. For a walk.

(She puts on her coat.)

RACHEL. Where?

SHEILA. Out.

JULIUS. I can –

RACHEL. Get away from her.

SHEILA. Be quiet. Both of you.

*(**SHEILA** exits the room, closing the door behind her. **RACHEL** and **JULIUS** stare at each other. After a moment, **RACHEL** moves to the corner of the room and props herself on a chair there like a gargoyle trying to steel herself.)*

JULIUS. I feel as though I've just been scolded and sent to the corner.

*(**RACHEL** says nothing.)*

Where do you suppose she's going?

RACHEL. Like she said, Out. She'll probably just walk around the grounds. It's nice out.

JULIUS. *(Nods. There's an uncomfortable pause.)* It's a good feeling, isn't it? To be able to come here and take care of her.

RACHEL. No.

JULIUS. Well, I'm sure you would rather she wasn't sick. But there's a part of you that feels vindicated.

RACHEL. What are you talking about?

JULIUS. You finally have her attention. She finally needs you. It always feels good to be needed.

RACHEL. You don't know anything about us.

JULIUS. Oh, I think I know a great deal. At first, the patient needs the nurse, but in the end, it is the nurse who needs the patient.

RACHEL. Spare me the psycho babble, okay? You come in here and put all these crazy ideas in my mother's head. –

JULIUS. What do you mean?

RACHEL. It's like she's become a different person.

JULIUS. She is. She's born again.

RACHEL. Oh please, I know your kind. You prey on helpless individuals who have no hope.

JULIUS. We provide a service. And in the modern world, it is how the church raises funds and how we continue to do good works and –

RACHEL. And line your own pockets, laughing all the way to the bank.

JULIUS. Your mother wrote to me.

RACHEL. So what? She's helpless and she doesn't know any better.

JULIUS. Oh really.

RACHEL. What did you promise her?

JULIUS. Nothing.

RACHEL. Come on. You must have spun her some kind of line.

JULIUS. I am beginning to feel very sorry for you.

RACHEL. Good. Why don't you feel sorry for me all the way back to California, okay? Just leave us in peace.

JULIUS. Sheila is coming with me.

RACHEL. What?

JULIUS. She's coming back to California with me.

RACHEL. What are you talking about?

JULIUS. She wants to get away from this place so she can start living again.

RACHEL. Okay. I don't know what kind of lies you've been telling her, but you're going to pack up your things and get the hell out of here.

JULIUS. Your mother's agreed to it.

RACHEL. When did she say that?

JULIUS. Just this morning. She has decided to leave here and spend her final days with me at the Heritage Ministries.

RACHEL. That is such bullshit.

(**SHEILA** *appears in the doorway.*)

JULIUS. Sheila.

SHEILA. It's too cold out.

RACHEL. Sit down, Ma.

SHEILA. I'm all right. Rachel, we need to talk –

RACHEL. Ma, this guy's telling me that you're going to leave the hospice and go back with him to California. I mean, come on, would you please –

SHEILA. I haven't decided that yet.

JULIUS. I know. I'm sorry, I was trying to explain –

RACHEL. What?

JULIUS. – to her that you were still considering the issue, but that I thought for certain that you –

RACHEL. What!?

JULIUS. *(pause)* Well.

RACHEL. I can't…I cannot believe this.

SHEILA. This is what I wanted to talk to you about. I'm thinking…I'm just going to go check it out. If I don't like it, I'll come back.

RACHEL. Ma –

SHEILA. And if I decide to stay for good, you can come visit me.

RACHEL. Don't you see what he's doing? He doesn't give a shit about you. All he wants is your money. He wants to get you out there so you'll start signing away your life savings to him and his friggin' church.

SHEILA. I would never do that.

RACHEL. He'll make you do that. That's what he's about, don't you understand?

SHEILA. This has nothing to do with money.

RACHEL. Of course it does. That's the only reason he's here.

JULIUS. I think I had better –

SHEILA. No, Julius. Stay.

RACHEL. *(to* JULIUS*)* Who the hell are you anyway? Who do you think you are to come in here and ruin everything?

SHEILA. Rachel.

RACHEL. I won't let you.

SHEILA. Listen to me.

RACHEL. Do you hear me? I WON'T LET YOU!

SHEILA. All right. Let's just settle this. Julius, I would love to come and live with you at the Heritage Ministries. But my daughter here is convinced that the only reason you have extended this invitation is because of my sizable bankbook. So would you please make it clear that your kindness is not contingent upon my making a donation?

JULIUS. What do you mean?

SHEILA. I mean, if I decided not to make a donation, you still would be more than happy to take me at the Heritage Ministries as your guest. Am I correct?

JULIUS. Well…

RACHEL. See?

SHEILA. Quiet. Am I correct?

JULIUS. Of course. Money has nothing to do with it.

RACHEL. Do you do this for all your followers.

JULIUS. No. Just the special ones.

*(***RACHEL** *grabs her coat and goes to the door.)*

SHEILA. Honey.

RACHEL. I'm leaving.

SHEILA. I'm not going right away.

RACHEL. That's all right. Send me a post card. I don't know what it is you're doing. But I'm going to find out.

(She exits.)

JULIUS. *(pause)* I'm sorry.

SHEILA. For what?

JULIUS. I didn't mean to cause so much trouble.

SHEILA. It was a long time coming. We never saw eye to eye on a lot of things. I just…I wish she understood things a little better.

JULIUS. That might be a bit too much to ask.

SHEILA. Maybe we should leave right away.

JULIUS. I was thinking the same thing.

SHEILA. How soon?

JULIUS. We could be on a plane tomorrow.

SHEILA. Really?

JULIUS. Really.

(He takes her shoulders.)

And begin a whole new chapter of your life.

(They kiss.)

The greatest part of all.

(Blackout)

Scene Three

(The next morning. JULIUS sits at the foot of the bed. He has his overcoat on and is ready to go. SHEILA stands between two open suitcases. She's making final preparations to leave.)

JULIUS. Take your time.

SHEILA. Haven't heard that in a while.

JULIUS. You have all the time in the world.

SHEILA. Do I?

JULIUS. Of course.

SHEILA. When is the car getting here?

JULIUS. Soon. I told him eleven. So ten minutes or so.

(pause)

Are you excited?

SHEILA. You know I am. It's like an adventure, you know? Do you think it's the right thing?

JULIUS. Of course. And no one says you have to stay. Just see what it's like and –

SHEILA. I feel bad about Rachel.

JULIUS. She'll be okay. You watch, she'll come visit you. We're talking about *your* life now.

SHEILA. I was thinking last night of how insane all of this is. I mean, if you told me a week ago I would be packing up out of here to go live out my life with an evangelist that I met on television I would have said –

JULIUS. You're not ready to quit yet. Are you?

SHEILA. No. I'm not.

JULIUS. Good. So let's go.

SHEILA. *(pointing to the suitcases)* Can I bring both of these?

JULIUS. Of course.

SHEILA. Are you sure –

JULIUS. What.

SHEILA. That…they'll be ready for me.

JULIUS. I was on the phone all last night making sure everything was arranged.

SHEILA. Uh-huh.

JULIUS. It's a great thing you're doing.

SHEILA. I know.

JULIUS. Time to leave.

(She closes up her suitcases, **JULIUS** *takes them up.)*

SHEILA. Is the car here?

JULIUS. We can wait outside.

SHEILA. I should call Rachel.

JULIUS. Didn't you call her last night?

SHEILA. She didn't answer.

JULIUS. Try her again from the airport.

SHEILA. I don't –

JULIUS. It is she who should be calling you. You are taking a step toward the light. She wants you to stay here and wallow in the misery of the dead and dying. Is that what you want? Is that why you wrote to me?

(They kiss. **RACHEL** *enters and stands in the doorway.* **SHEILA** *notices her and pulls away.)*

RACHEL. Well. I guess it's not about the money, huh.

JULIUS. Good morning.

SHEILA. I've been calling you.

RACHEL. I wasn't answering the phone.

SHEILA. Oh. Where were you?

RACHEL. I went to the law office. I had to work on some things before I came over.

SHEILA. Wait, who said you could do that?

RACHEL. It had nothing to do with you.

JULIUS. I'm going to take these out to the car.

RACHEL. You're staying right here.

SHEILA. We were just about to leave.

RACHEL. So what are you, like a couple now?

JULIUS. It would seem so.

RACHEL. I thought you were on a religious…quest. I thought fine. Your religion failed you. But this is ridiculous.

SHEILA. What, I'm tool old to fall in love?

RACHEL. I didn't say that.

SHEILA. Well what then?

RACHEL. It has nothing to do with looking for a way to help you…

SHEILA. Say it.

RACHEL. It has to do with getting your rocks off at the end of your life.

SHEILA. Oh please.

RACHEL. And losing your family and your life savings in the process.

SHEILA. So what am I supposed to do? Sit here and wait for death to come?

RACHEL. No, you can do whatever you want.

SHEILA. That's right. I can and I will. And you're not going to stop me, you understand? I already told you, this has nothing to do with money.

JULIUS. Sheila –

SHEILA. And I'm not changing my mind!

JULIUS. – you're getting all upset over nothing.

SHEILA. I know. Okay.

(to RACHEL)

Do you think you'll be coming out to visit me?

RACHEL. Do you think you'll ever support what I do? Do you think you'll have respect for my choices?

SHEILA. I do. And I have for your entire life.

RACHEL. Really?

SHEILA. Yes.

RACHEL. *(to SHEILA)* Okay.

(pause)

(to JULIUS) What's Wrath of Angels?

JULIUS. Excuse me?

RACHEL. You heard what I said.

JULIUS. I don't know what you're talking about.

RACHEL. You know, I couldn't quite place you. And then I googled you and I saw your website and all the great things that you do and I checked out a lot of other links, but there was no direct connection. And then this morning I was in Barbara's office, cause they have access to legal documents and sites that are on the FBI's watch list; and right there everything fell into place.

JULIUS. FBI watch list? What are you –

RACHEL. "Wrath of Angels" is a division of the Right to Life Militancy Network. They fund people who bomb abortion clinics.

(RACHEL looks directly at SHEILA.)

JULIUS. I don't know of any militancy network –

RACHEL. Maybe next time you're talking to my mother about all the work you do, you can tell her about that little sideshow. How do you suppose she'd feel about that?

JULIUS. Where are you getting these crazy ideas?

RACHEL *(overlapping)* Abortion Clinics, right? You know what those are, right?

JULIUS. Yes, I know what an abortion clinic is.

RACHEL *(overlapping)* I saw it with my own eyes, Ma.

JULIUS. And I do not condone the bombing of abortion clinics.

RACHEL. No, you just give people money so they can buy the weapons to bomb the abortion clinics.

SHEILA. Rachel!

RACHEL. Then you put up a website with people's names on it crossed out like it's some kind of virtual game of Dungeons and Dragons. The only difference is, when people get crossed out in this game, they don't come back.

JULIUS. We have never used money for that purpose. We spread the word of the Lord. Everything we do is in his name! Sheila, do you think for one minute I could take your money and use it to commit acts of violence?

RACHEL. That is exactly what I think!

JULIUS *(overlapping)* Young lady, I think you've been –

RACHEL *(overlapping)* Don't "young lady" me!

JULIUS. – spending too much time on the internet researching conspiracy theories.

RACHEL. My name is on that list!

JULIUS. What list? There's no list.

RACHEL. Don't fuck with me. I saw it.

JULIUS. I don't know of any list! How could I have anything do with your name being on a list when I just met you?

RACHEL. Barbara saw it. She saw the site.

JULIUS. Who's Barbara?

RACHEL. My mother's lawyer. We both saw the whole thing this morning.

JULIUS. All right, I am not going to stand here and listen to you spread lies about me or my ministry.

RACHEL. You like being a charmer, don't you?

JULIUS. Sheila, we have a plane to catch.

RACHEL *(in his face)* You get off on this.

JULIUS *(to RACHEL)* Have a good time with all your crazy ideas.

RACHEL. How does it feel to have blood on your hands?

JULIUS. You stop that.

RACHEL. How does it feel to be a murderer?

JULIUS. Abortion is murder!

RACHEL. Oh really?

JULIUS. The endless massacre of the unborn!

RACHEL. I thought you had nothing to do with it.

JULIUS *(calming himself)* I don't. I have nothing to do with the bombing of abortion clinics.

RACHEL. It's bad enough you're trying to take my mother's money, but now I find out you're giving it to a right wing fringe group that's trying to kill me while I'm at work. .

JULIUS *(overlapping)* That is a lie! I have nothing to do with this!

RACHEL. Why don't you kill me right now? You can scratch another abortionist off the list!

SHEILA. Stop! Both of you.

(After a pause, she looks to JULIUS.)

What about this?

JULIUS. It isn't true.

RACHEL. Mom, you can ask Barbara.

JULIUS. I told you, I don't know what she's talking about. Now are you coming with me?

RACHEL. Call her, she saw it too. She saw the whole thing.

JULIUS. It is a complete falsehood.

RACHEL. Call her Mom.

JULIUS. Yeah. Go ahead and call her.

RACHEL. Here.

JULIUS. Give it to me. I'll speak to her directly.

RACHEL. Get out of here.

*(He grabs **RACHEL**'s wrist, hurting her. **RACHEL** pulls away.)*

JULIUS. Give me the phone!

RACHEL. Get your fucking hands off me!

JULIUS. Give it to me!

SHEILA. Rachel!

RACHEL (overlapping) Shit! Ow, you bastard!

JULIUS (overlapping) I'm sorry.

RACHEL. Sonovabitch.

*(**RACHEL** clutches her wrist in pain...anything to turn the tables on **JULIUS**.)*

JULIUS. I didn't mean to –

RACHEL. Get the fuck away from me.

JULIUS. It was an accident.

RACHEL. Get your ass out of here before I call the cops.

JULIUS. Sheila, she's making this whole thing up. She's trying to come between us.

RACHEL. *(to* **SHEILA***)* What are you gonna do when my name gets crossed out?

(pause as **SHEILA** *looks to* **JULIUS** *and then* **RACHEL***)*

SHEILA. *(Long pause.* **SHEILA** *answers, but does not sound convinced.)* I can't.

JULIUS. But…you were all ready to leave.

SHEILA. I know.

JULIUS. You said –

SHEILA. I know. I can't.

JULIUS. But nothing's changed. Why won't you believe me?

SHEILA. *(She closes her eyes and answers, almost as if trying to remember who she is and what she believes.)* I don't know what to believe. When I'm with you, I feel…strong. I feel invincible. Like I could live forever. But I can't simply change everything just because you give me a new set of stories about an afterlife that I've never believed in. It's not who I am. I'm Jewish.

JULIUS. I thought your religion abandoned you.

SHEILA. No. I abandoned my religion. And I can't abandon my family. Not now.

JULIUS. Sheila, you've made me think about things in a whole new way.

SHEILA. She's my daughter.

JULIUS. I need you.

SHEILA. And if anything ever happened to her –

JULIUS. She's lying!

SHEILA. I don't know what I would do.

JULIUS. *(pause)* All right. Fine. I thought….Fine. None of this is true. None of it.

(He takes out the pen she gave him and places it on the table.)

God bless you both.

(He exits. The two stand there in shock, for a long quiet moment.)

RACHEL. I'm sorry, Ma.

SHEILA. Don't say anything.

RACHEL. *(She fights back the tears.)* I'm sorry I ruined it.

SHEILA. Stop it.

RACHEL. I didn't mean to –

SHEILA. Stop.

(pause)

It wouldn't work anyway. And I could never live with myself knowing where the money was going.

(pause)

But…he made me happy.

RACHEL. I thought you were going to go with him.

SHEILA. Well I didn't.

RACHEL. I'm sorry I'm such a disappointment to you.

SHEILA. No.

RACHEL. I am.

(The two hug, but are still uneasy with each other.)

SHEILA. Rachel, please…

*(**SHEILA** just wants to get through the conversation. **RACHEL** is a disappointment to her and perhaps always will be.)*

RACHEL. You wanted me to be someone else. But I'm not and I never will be.

SHEILA. I know. I didn't think you were ever like me.

RACHEL. No?

*(**SHEILA** shakes her head, no.)*

You should eat something.

SHEILA. I don't feel like it.

RACHEL. I'll make you a pipe.

SHEILA. No. I just want to sit.

RACHEL. Okay.

(**RACHEL** *goes to the foyer hangs* **SHEILA**'s *coat.*)

SHEILA. You're right you would have run the business into the ground.

RACHEL. You think?

SHEILA. You have to be ruthless. You have to bend the truth…it's just not in you.

(*pause*)

You know, it's funny, I had forgotten what it was like to be that close to somebody. And it's almost as if that closeness reminded me of what real isolation feels like. To just be in one place by yourself. And it's okay. Because everybody has to go through it. And maybe… maybe I'm ready.

(*pause*)

Thanks for taking care of me.

RACHEL. I love taking care of you Mom.

SHEILA. Can you put the TV on?

RACHEL. Sure.

SHEILA. I'm going to watch a little and then I'm going to take a nap.

(**SHEILA** *closes her eyes.* **RACHEL** *grabs the flicker and turns on the TV. We hear the voice of* **JULIUS STRONG** *preaching.*)

JULIUS. (*V.O.*) "What is the greatest love? The greatest love of all is from our Savior Jesus Christ"

RACHEL. Well. That was quick.

SHEILA. Must be a repeat.

RACHEL. Must be.

(**RACHEL** *goes to the TV and then hesitates.*)

How does he get that Bible to stay open?

SHEILA. *(with irony)* It's a trick.

RACHEL. I'll bet.

SHEILA. Can you change the channel?

RACHEL. Sure.

JULIUS. *(V.O.)* "But how do we gain this love, brother and sisters"

(**RACHEL** *mutes it and grabs a stack of magazines from the side table and begins cleaning up.*)

SHEILA. So tired. I should call Barbara tomorrow.

RACHEL. What for?

SHEILA. She shouldn't make those changes.

RACHEL. Oh don't worry about it, I'll call her when she gets back from vacation.

SHEILA. *(pause)* You said you saw her today.

RACHEL. Hm?

SHEILA. You said you saw Barbara today. At the office.

RACHEL. I did.

SHEILA. I thought…didn't you say she was going to fly out last night?

RACHEL. She's leaving this afternoon.

(**RACHEL** *and* **SHEILA** *exchange a long look. It's as if the two are seeing each other for the first time.* **RACHEL** *goes to* **SHEILA** *and removes her wig.* **SHEILA** *continues to stare at her daughter.*)

Close your eyes.

(**SHEILA** *nods and turns away,* **RACHEL** *continues.*)

SHEILA. *(quietly)* Don't leave me.

RACHEL. I won't.

(**RACHEL** *takes her hand. She then strokes her face.*)

SHEILA. *(quietly, as if trying to soothe herself)* I dreamt of Amelia Earhardt. So strong. All alone in the sky, needing no one else. And then washed away….

RACHEL. Shhh.

SHEILA. Like a broken bird that crashed into the sea.

RACHEL. Don't worry Mom. I won't leave you.

(Pause. **SHEILA** *smiles and closes her eyes.)*

I'll take care of everything.

*(***RACHEL** *leans over and kisses her mother on the forehead.*

JULIUS. *(V.O.)* "What kind of love is it? Is it the kind of love that would make you steal? Is it the kind of love that would make you lie? Is it the kind of love – "

End of Play

From the Reviews of
APOSTASY...

"When Sheila Gold announces to her grown daughter, Rachel, that she is thinking of trading in her barely used Judaism for late-model, born-again Christianity, it looks as if we're being set up for a play about religious faith. But Gino DiIorio has something else up his sleeve in *Apostasy*, the absorbing new drama. Sheila's flirtation with Jesus is going to turn into a flirtation of an entirely different kind. And abortion politics will intrude messily on the play's relationships...

...Mr. DiIorio's fearless play, first staged last year at the New Jersey Repertory Company in Long Branch, is more than a soap opera. He weaves in compelling exchanges on issues of faith. Julius's unorthodox explanation of how he views his job is especially delicious."
- *The New York Times*

"Race, faith, money, betrayal, abortion, nudity, terminal illness, medical marijuana, middle-age sex...a button-pusher that seeks to provoke a reaction at every turn, even as it foils most attempts to predict plotlines and pigeonhole motivations."
- *Asbury Park Press*

"Playwright Gino DiIorio pairs a terminally ill Jewish businesswoman with a charismatic black Christian televangelist, in a star-crossed love affair that raises questions about faith, self-deception, and what happens when we die."
- *NJN*

www.ingramcontent.com/pod-product-compliance
Lightning Source LLC
Chambersburg PA
CBHW070647300426
44111CB00013B/2315